Siege Of Canterbury
Millennial Creative Writing Competition

Commissioned poems and shortlisted entries

S@ve As Writers' Group

Published by Save As Publishers

Introduction

ISBN-13:   978-0-9929473-1-6

Consultancy, Formatting, Graphics and Cover Design by

www.hotmonkeypublishing.com

CONTENTS

Introduction

In 2010 Frederic Stansfield, a fellow SaveAs Writers' member, informed me that the following year, 2011, would see the 1000th anniversary of the Siege of Canterbury. Fred is very informed on the subject matter and was adamant that this significant event in the city's history should be commemorated. I, on the other hand, knew next to nothing about it so I researched the subject further. Eventually, as a Canterbury-based group, it was felt that SaveAs Writers had an obligation to the city and this is how the Siege of Canterbury Millennial Creative Writing Competition came about.

So in 2011 entries were invited in both prose and poetry based around the siege and subsequent sack of the city by the Vikings. Although the subject was very much unique to Kent, the competition was open internationally and entries were received from other continents. In addition three accomplished local poets were commissioned to write new poems based on the event. These were premiered at the Awards evening which formed part of the Canterbury Festival (and I wish to thank the Festival for helping to make the competition possible.)

This anthology consists of the three commissioned poems and the shortlisted works in both categories. What makes this book so remarkable, in my opinion, isn't just the quality of the writing but the diverse ways the writers have broached the theme. Further, the events of that torrid time are so vividly portrayed that the layman could read this book and receive a very comprehensive but concise history lesson.

I don't want to say any more about the contents of the book because I would be unable to do them justice; and I want this introduction to be as short as possible so you, and I, can turn the page and read on as quickly as possible. But before you do can I thank Christopher Hobday for helping me judge the competition; the Festival for helping the book get published; the commissioned poets – Jan Montefiore, Nancy Gaffield and Maggie Harris – for their dedication to the task. A very big thank you to Jeremy Dunhill and Hot Monkey Publishing for putting the book together – without them it would never have come to fruition. Last but not least, I would like to thank all of Saves Writers for their support, and all of the entrants to the competition because without you there would have been no book for us to publish.

I hope you enjoy the book – I think you will – and, whilst reading, remember that what you are holding is not only an anthology of superb writing but a remembrance of the historic events of 1000 years ago.

Luigi Marchini, Chair of SaveAs Writers' group

Abecedarian Hymn For St Alphege
by Nancy Gaffield

Anglo-Saxon Chronicles record the facts:
Archbishop AElfheah taken captive
A thousand years ago. The riders of the sea-steed
    bore down with
Axes flaying flesh from bone.

Begin now your labour of death
Between the Nativity of St Mary and Michaelmas.

Birds in flight absorbed the sky
    the cast of blood and
Blackened corn. Clamour of cracking
Bones rent the air, ashes rose from
Burnt out houses, timbers scorched.
Cantwaraburg lost
    our sacred heart,
Cathedral Church of Christ.
Children captured as slaves, or if too young to,
    murdered in their beds.

City of bliss was gone.

Cloaked in the assassin's weeds
Dane AElfmaer came and slashed their weald.
Darkness brayed within him,
Death and destruction his art, and he
Did it very well. Fathers implored children to hide
Dig a hole in the floor,
Dissolve amongst cowslips and ivy.
Do not stir beneath the feet that trample you.
Each day I will return to find you
    but returning he found
Emptiness instead.

Even the tombs bloom with rue.
Faces frozen in slivers of glass
Fade in the distance of each passing year.
For them I sing this
Gnostic hymn.

Havoc and horrors heave them into battle
He is shouldered away
Heart-broken and humiliated
    survivors scatter
Helter-skelter they wander from this world to the next,
Hunted across pasture to smouldering woods.

In the rupture of this far-flung
Instant fashioned in shards of glass
    I too am in the fray, though
It is summer here and torrential rain
    pelts the roof.

Journey of a thousand years.

Kneeling before this ancient window
Knowing with a knowledge that burns thought away,
    pray
Let this cup pass,
    cross the dark matter to read
Messages from their time
Millennium slaughter englobed in glass
    seven hundred years ago.

Near here is a river the elders named
    Fisbourne Stream. It enters the sea
    at Wantsum Channel and the Isle of Thanet.
    Under the dome of night
No Spear-Dane could reach them there,
    disgorge them from their earth-fort
Now they would be safe
On the riverbank where green grow the rushes to
Open sea where they took him upriver
Our most sacred saint

and pelted him to brutal death
    those Danish men with
Oxen bones.

Past and present collide:
    the consonance of the Anglo-Saxon world
    simultaneous though distorted
Pillars interject their own uncertainty
Quiet broken by a modern English prayer
    the colouring less intense
Reflected in sun-cloaked hues of rose and blue
    the rain has stopped some light pouring through
Resurrecting you from the shadows
    outside marauding crows
    perch in the yews.

Rising from my pew I see the unremitting Danes
    move out of dream and into the lintels
    ripping door from hinge
Sacking the town till only embers remained.
    Our bright
Sanctuary turned to kindling and smoke.

Searching for what would never be found
She buries her face in cypress bough.
She follows the others down to the sea
    all reason gone
She skims the surface
    of her grief, dives down
Swims low, how fast
    life ebbs away.

    The air breathes me
    The breath a simple scratch
        catch of a burr on deer skin
    The dear departed are waving to us through the rowan trees
    The ear forgives the wind
        features are lost from the edges
        forgotten children buried in epochs

gulf between backwards and forwards
The hour beyond
    irrational velocity of time
    jack of all trades (master of none)
The kites ride the updraft searching for meat
The lap of a wave mimics a lullaby
    mothers used to sing
The new barbarity comes in the throwing
    of oxen bones
The open eye that beholds the wheel turning
    perpetual and furious trouble to see things clearly
    quiet gradation of light on the horizon
The randomness of it
    skylark and song
    somniis meis fis—
you become because of my dreams
Truth remains a fable
The universal past yawns
The voice slips into the forest amongst hornbeams
    woman great with child buried in reeds
The x that equals no, nobody, nothing, nowhere
    you I see slipping away
The zodiacal sign of the moon

Time grows dark then darker
Unuttered prayers fall on deaf ears,
Vanishing in coils of frankincense.

Walking in the streets of Canterbury
Was I not always dreaming you into existence?

With your white hair streaming?
X'd from the record, except for this window;
    figures
Yoked in time.
Zyxt: obsolete Kentish word
    unwinding the clock,
      crossing the sea, retracing your steps,

Siege Of Canterbury

I find you
in leaded panes twice removed
hearing the rain again.

The Death Of Ælfheah
by Jan Montefiore

I call the archbishop Ælfheah because that was his name. Alphege is a later, Latinised version. The first syllable of Ælfheah is pronounced "Alf".

The poem's metre is based on the four-stress Old English alliterative line, though not all of my own lines alliterate. It includes translated quotations from Ælfric's life of St Edmund the king of East Anglia who was martyred by Viking invaders about 200 years before Ælfheah; from the Old English poem 'The Wanderer'; and from the account in the *Anglo-Saxon Chronicle* of the 1011 Danish invasion of England and the imposition of "Dane-geld', as it was later known. The story of Bjarki finding the man in the bone-pile comes from the Old Norse saga *Hrolf Kraki* about the Danish King Hrolf, a legendary figure from the mid-6th century AD. The description of winter food shortages and famine conditions in pre-modern Europe are quoted from Dorothy Hartley's *Food In England* (1954).

The last third of the poem twice quotes my free translation of the 'Death Song' chanted on his death-bed by the great Northumbrian historian Bede in the 8th century AD:

> Fore there neidfaerae naenig uuiurthit
> thoncsnotturra than him tharf sie
> to ymbhycggannae   aer his hiniongae
> huaet his gastae   godaes aeththa yflaes
> aefter deothdaege   doemid uueorthae.

"Until that destined journey, no man is wiser than he needs to be to consider, before he goes hence, to what his soul will be doomed after death, good or evil."

When the Danes came to Kent at Michaelmas
plundering and slaying, as their custom is
they laid siege to Canterbury and sacked the city,

seizing for ransom archbishop Ælfheah,
Abbess Leofrune, lesser monks and priests
laymen and women, *too many to count,*

and after taking every profitable captive
they left in November with archbishop Ælfheah,
pricing his freedom at a million silver pennies.

Winter was near, a harsh time for natives,
the green food gone from woods and commons,
the corn all cut, the wild fruits finished,

pigs that had pastured on beech mast and acorns
slaughtered and salted, leaving a few
beasts for breeding: little to live on.

But for warriors of the winning army
the season meant ale, the feast laid ready,
the joys of the hall, the bright cup, the treasure-giver

and the drunken games of munching meat
and throwing bones at unlucky victims,
like the weakling whom once the hero Bjarki

found hiding in the hall of King Hrolf the Dane
in a heap of gnawed bones with one blackened hand
sticking out. Bjarki took it and pulled out a man

scrawny and stinking, who screamed in terror
"Do you want to kill me ? You wrecked my bone-pile,
my only defence from drunkards at dinner.

Now I have nothing, no safety left."
But when a guest threw a great ox thigh-bone
Bjarki sent it back, smashing his skull,

dragged out the weakling, made him wash
off the bone-stink, and gave him the blood of dragon
to drink, which turned him into a hero

and he fought alongside Bjarki defending King Hrolf
against his witch-sister, till the two died in battle
after which none can say what befell them

for no one knows before he is forced
to his final journey, to what his soul
will be doomed after death, good or evil.

Archbishop Ælfheah, English churchman,
was not like Bjarki fighting and slaying
bullies at meat. He drank no blood

nor struck with a sword, he raised his hands
only in blessing of water or wine.
And the hands were empty as his people's purses

that year when the English were paying Dane-geld,
ten million pennies of protection money
already taxed from the English people.

For a further million, the folk of Kent
must sell their horses, their oxen and seed-corn.
Then famine would follow, that terrible time

when lacking plough beasts, no fields can be tilled
and men hunt for roots or gather acorns
for a wretched ash-cake, snakes, snails, anything,

the last beast slaughtered, no hope left.
So Ælfheah *forbade that any man should sell
goods for his sake.* And the Danes were angry.

Feasting and merry on wine from the south,
they seized the archbishop and struck him with bones
and heads of oxen they hurled by the horns,

and at last took an axe to smash his skull
*and his holy blood ran down to the earth
and his holy spirit went up to God's kingdom*

where no one knows before he is forced
to his final journey, to what his soul
will be doomed after death, good or evil.

Sea, Ship, Wall, Stone
by Maggie Harris

Letter from Ivar's wife, Aestrid to her mother, 1009:

Dear Mother the day now comes, the blackest day, the brightest
   day
For I must put smile upon my countenance and wave our
   Banner gold and high
For hereforth my Lord goes forth brave and bold to face great
      dragons, on both land and sea
Here I wait and here I pray our gods protect and honor He
Who takes his life across a sea to face the savage; carry he our
      wisdom and our lightenment
Sea, ship, wall, stone. Sea, ship, wall, stone.

Song of the mid-current:

   Hasten thee, o hasten thee, o wooden prow
O Viking lea, two thousand arms are rowing strong
      to cross my bitter northern sea
Leave now these lands of rock and ice
      That hath no earth to bind your feet
      Your angry kinsmen turn on thee
      And send you forth, to banquish thee
      To cross my bitter northern sea
      For land and hopeful powerment
Sea, ship, wall stone. Sea, ship, wall, stone.

Song of the Kent Coast:

   It came as a whisper on the wind
   To those who trawled their nets
   To those who tended sheep
   To those who gathered wheat
   The scent of Norse men;
   The sound of stamping feet.

All gathered their children
One moment one time one woman's cry
One child, one son, one hand held to the throat
Sea, ship, wall, stone. Sea, ship, wall, stone.

Unknown scribe of the city:

The wall, our wall, with its heart of stone, stood resolute
Those citizens of whom we may not know, stood fast upon it.
Our wall we had built with blood and stone
That wall of Roman bones, our Christian souls
    face to the North Wind –
That wall of earthernware feet, its tombstones of breastplate
    and copper
its bronze hair-pieces filleted into the earth
sleeping their timeless sleep
turning in dreams they dreamed, of those who had come this
    way before
that wall, our wall ... of such tragedy I can not speak ...
Sea, ship, wall, stone. Sea, ship, wall, stone.

The shepherd on the meadow caught the scent of strangers
The sheep turned their petrified eyes to a horizon gap-toothed
    with gorse and flint, tumps of earth and apple bough
The nuns in their nunnery lifted their pale faces up to an
    empty sky seeking the arms of the Almighty, preparing
    their souls for the final journey
Anything that bore passage moved; each horse, each cart, each
    mule, each litter, each craft of skin and oak, took to fields
    and rivers, slid into the Stour, scrambled hedge, sought
    cave, became a marketplace of moving souls
Each creature that had wing took wing
Each that had hoof took hoof

Each that roamed meadows sought the gully, the dam, the
    shelter of farm
Each wild thing heard the cry, each ear the stamping soles, the
    thump of heel on mud and stone
Sea, ship, wall, stone ...

And men will write much of that day
When in that great city, Canterbury
Tales ran like blood, of such which I cannot speak
But from which Saints were made

And Aestred, like all women wait
And pen their songs of loss –

My lover sails, my husband brave,
Soon he will set sail for home
Sea, ship, wall, stone. Sea, ship, wall, stone.

The Siege Of Canterbury: Three Voices
by Derek Sellen

AELFMAER:
Oxbone and axehead, they martyred our Alphege,
with fire and slaughter they hollowed our city.
I was the one who led them to unguarded ways
and earned myself the name of traitor.
I was a necessity of the plot, the key to it all:
every Christ demands a Judas. I was he.
Do you blame me, as our ribs grew sharper,
while they roasted our sheep in range of our nostrils
and fished the water meadows? Would they ever
have departed or simply waited out our deaths?

Who gained in the end? What endures?
        Wrecking and looting doesn't make
a pretty picture though it might satisfy the moment.
A holy man, frail and aged, herded onto a ship,
opposing prayer to the jeers of bulky warriors.
Oxbone and axehead, they martyred our Alphege.
They won the siege. But we have the better story.

THE DANES:
We are the men of the sea, we ride on the swell;
they dwell within walls and that is their weakness.
It wasn't difficult to sniff out a traitor, a heart
that had rotted in closed places stinking of envy.
We released him, the Abbott Aelfmaer, with smiles
though he begged us not to. He wanted it secret,
he expected discretion. But we gained pleasure
in tossing him overboard, trussed in his own treachery.

A better story? What's better than valour
and skill in battle? So what if the old man
wasn't worth a ransom, perhaps he was as tiresome
to them as he was to us. A sermonising hostage,
who wants him? The oxbone was the best solution.

Let them remember their Alphege in a book of tales;
we are the men of the sea, we ride on the swell,
the wave and the wind are what we read, the stars narrate.

A WOMAN:
You are born of the salt and born of the sword,
the bastard war-spawn
      – the story-tellers would say –
         of one of the women.
We're not bishops or warriors; that we kept the city
through ninety days of siege is unimportant.
To be devout, to wail in chorus when things go badly,
to dress the wounds and make meals out of nothing,
that is our role, tucked in the margins of windy sagas.

A longship beached its prow in the shingle,
in a screech of gulls he planted his foot on the land;
this armoured thing
      – I will not call him a man –
         hunted me down
and left me bloodied with his seed in my womb.
His bards approve. It makes him a hero.
Thank God for the hag who dragged me out of the dust
before a second one found me. She soothed me of terror.
You are born of the salt and born of the sword, my son,
you will do great deeds;
      but none as great as the women of Canterbury's.

Scriptorium
by Marilyn Donovan

> *Then the Lord said unto me, Out of the North an evil shall break forth upon all the inhabitants of the land.*
> On halgum gewritum Jeremiah 1:14

Ianuarius, 1011

Brother Ælfric hunches over the slope of his desk, its massy oak scraped nearer a frost-bowered window to catch the fading light. His quill is sharp but his hands are blunted with cold, the minuscule marching across the *bócfell* grown erratic. His ink has frozen several times; he had had to hold the horn over his candle's wavering flame to thaw, the scent of oak gall, vinegar, green vitriol slashing the gelid air.

To divert the brothers from their wretchedness he has angled his hands at Athelstan, bidding him read from the holy Bible. The room is silent save for his voice, stumbling often as the words slide in the skinny light, and the creak of men shifting position to relieve rheumatic cramps.

They say Hell is cold as an iron blade.

He has set the novices to manual tasks, hoping the movement will speed blood flowing sluggish through winter veins. Dunstan is measuring and pricking quires ready to rule, his features sharpened by the cold, a drop of moisture hanging from his nose. Eadfrith is shaping good goose feathers into *hearpenglas*. One floor below Ethelwold, the most trustworthy, is blending *blæc*. Ælfric imagines him holding chilblain-swollen fingers to the feeble heat warming the alembic.

Behind him, Brother Wulfstan is scraping calfskin clean of ink to use again, his breath rasping with concentration, his left hand bound in a bloody rag. A sharp hiss through blackened teeth from time to time marks the blade slipping, gouging the vellum. Ælfric signals him to stop, it is dangerous in this cold, the fell is too resistant, and he sets down the knife, slides numbed hands inside the folds of his sleeves, bows his head to the flow of the reading.

Soon the great bell will chime vespers and they will all lay aside their tools to shuffle into the cathedral, glad of the exercise. It is many years since such a winter, three long months already of a cold as hard as flint. Surely they must all have sinned greatly to merit it.

Ælfric is heavy in his heart. His is a silent order but news percolates in from the outer world and the brothers flutter details from finger to eye to mind, where it burrows like a worm into the heart of a rose. The Northmen have resumed their raids and Ethelred *cyning* is not stout in his courage, preferring to pay geld rather than standing fast to defend his people. He receives poor counsel from the *witan*, prevaricates, sues for peace too late, when the most harm has been inflicted.

They will not come in winter, will have withdrawn across the tossing sea to wait the cold out safe in their unholy homesteads. But come *sumerhát*... Canterbury holds out a tempting prize, its lands fat with sheep and cattle, its citizens prosperous, the cathedral rich in wrought plate, gold chalices, reliquaries, the great *godspel béc* (though he has heard the pagan hordes seek only to wrench away their wooden boards set with *fæt* and winking *eorcanstánas* of garnet, opal, amethyst, the holy writ inside useful only to serve their jakes).

His ink grows thick again. A day that never fully dawned is waning. Shadows deepen among the stone ribs and rough rafters overhead, where bats hibernate in a sooty clot that seems to breathe with its own life as they fidget in their sleep. The cold has dried him to a husk, hollowed out his entrails, leaving him empty as an abandoned bee's nest, his skin whorled and flaky as its tissue walls. Though he signals for more candles they burn but feebly, throwing jigging goblin shadows across the walls. The air is rancid

20

with frost and melted candle wax, lank hair and the stink of bodies long unwashed, the monks too weak from nights sleepless with cold to break the ice, apply vigour to their ablutions.

On days such as this he wishes he worked in the kitchens, ovens stoked, the warmth heady with the scent of braising meat, yeasty wine, fresh-baked bread. Or in the stables with their steaming straw and fleas and stamping horses, his head to the flank of a milch cow as he pulls the sweet milk slow and steady.

They say the Northmen know neither fear nor mercy, spit children on their swords. Even now, sconced in their hovels, they will be forging blades, sharpening axe and spear and *seax*, laying plans, braggarting success. The brothers are afraid; under cover of prayer their flapping hands whisper firedrakes and other superstitious portents.

It is half a lifetime since last *sumerhát*, when he moved his desk outdoors, sat under the trees to write, sunlight dripping through the tender leaves of oak and ash and cherry, pooling in fat gold coins on the short grass. Then he had felt young again, his blood up and coursing, hand and eye working effortlessly to draw out curlicues and arabesques, lay down rubrics, decorate the margins, his illuminating a fluid meditation on the glory of Creation. Once a tiny *gærshoppa* alighted on the corner of his desk, scraped out a brief tune before moving on.

The wax in his tablet had been soft, his *bócfell* supple as he pricked out the great Chi Rho. His pigments had flowed and dried as they should, the gold leaf had smoothed and cleaved. Now it is too cold to work the carpet designs, the elaborate initials, the six-winged symbols for Matthew, Mark, Luke and John, he is confined to endless scribing. He dreams of spring, when he can break free, loose the joy of cinnabar, verdigris, lapis lazuli, his whole body singing silent praise. Pray God they are working outside when the heathen come, can find a hole wherein to hide.

Cold slides from the walls, his feet now stones. When he stands he must take care not to stumble. Any minute now the even-bell will toll release from work. Ælfric lays down his quill in readiness, but not before dipping one more time to scribble in the margin:

A furore Normannorum libera nos, Domine!
From the fury of the Northmen, deliver us O Lord

Unready

by Sonia Overall

The great vaulting arch of a pause
hangs above us.
We wait.

For them, a day as any other:
spreading cloth on stones by the river,
stabling horses, tending beasts, bread
broken, fires banked with ash,
the mumbling of monks in the cloisters
marking another day behind broad stone walls,
mouthing of prayers
        and then to their beds

(no ships' planks for them, no dew on their blankets)

each dwelling on his day, his deeds,
the bargains and speeches,
some falling to with oaths on their lips,
others with necks bent, fingers worrying,
pouring into sleep as they will into death,
guilts and longings immutable as
pebbles on the tongue
        as mine are now

none knowing how soon they must be answered.

Yet we have our orders, our chiefs,
and each has his reason –
a badge to raise in the skirmish, a cause to rally to.
There will be gold, they say, and ransoms.
My blade is keen and polished.
Damp seeps into seam and joint
and the young men mutter
      will it ever be day?

The great church sits like a ripe fruit, ready to split.

I wrap my cloak about my feet
and watch for the thin line of morning
to turn and draw, an oiled bolt.
May it be done, and swiftly.

In The Enemy Camp
by Jo Field

He sits away from the fire, as far from the carousing as he is permitted to get, which probably isn't far enough. The night is the mildest yet, spring finally arrived, but his cloak is threadbare after more than half a year of constant wear and underneath it he wraps his arms across his chest and rubs bony shoulders.

"Hey old man!"

Alphege turns his smile on the drunkard.

"Old man, hey, give'sh a shtory!"

He shakes his head.

"You do not like my stories," he says. "I have the bruises to prove it."

More figures loom, black against the bright of the fire.

"*This* one has a tale to tell."

A stout man in a monk's scapula is thrust forward. Alphege narrows his eyes to peer up at him.

"If it's not my old friend Elfmar! And in the habit of a humble monk! How have you come here to Greenwich?"

"My lord Archbishop. Thank heaven you are safe."

"But what befell you during the slaying? The plundering and spoiling of our fated city? *You* are not dead I see."

"No no. I was ... suffered to leave Canterbury, and am lately now a captive like yourself."

"Thank the Lord you are alive at least. Having been preserved in the Great Famine it would otherwise be a shame."

"I am ever mindful of your intervention then on my behalf sir."

The Danes have lost interest, forgetting their craving for stories in the slaking of a more urgent thirst. They refill their cups with wine, lurching and slopping and singing. Elfmar, after glancing around in search of a better option, lowers himself to the rutted earth beside the archbishop, who beams a smile upon him.

"So, Abbot Elfmar, I trust your heart has been made more soft and kindly since your escape."

"My escape?"

"Since your deliverance from the anger of the peasants in the famine these six years gone. You have been generous now in sharing your blessings with them? You have learned the error of your ways?"

The other man bows his head.

"Indeed my lord. I have."

"And I am glad to hear it. When were you ... suffered to leave the city?"

"Shortly after yourself sir. With others who were spared."

"You are a fortunate man indeed. Heaven smiles on you." And so saying, the archbishop smiles on him too.

Elfmar makes his own face solemn and pious.

"We are none of us fortunate sir who witnessed the terror and the carnage of that time."

"You are right there my friend. It was the Devil's work."

"Satan has run unchecked through all of Kent. And Sussex,

Hastings …"

"Terrible times."

"Hampshire too I hear, and Surrey. Berkshire …"

"Terrible, terrible."

"Wiltshire. Not to mention those many shires north of the Thames." The abbot shakes his head sorrowfully over the extent of the carnage. "How such things come about is a mystery," he says, "under the eye of God."

"It is not for us to know how or why these horrors occur." Alphege is looking keenly at his companion. "But you are spared, and we may thank the good Lord for it."

"And you sir!" Elfmar cuts in. "You are spared too, by God's grace. But they say you will not let the people ransom you."

"The Lord knows where will be an end of it." The gentle smile persists on the archbishop's lips, albeit faded at the edges.

"A riddle!" It is a Danish cry. "Come, Black Monk. We need a riddle from you, or you will feel the kick of the ox." The man is brandishing a large bone, picked clean from the feasting.

"Know you any riddles, Abbot Elfmar?" Alphege asks.

Elfmar clambers to his feet with noticeable reluctance and is soon surrounded by a semicircle of expectant faces. Alphege nods benignly.

"Children," he says. "Simple children."

"My nose," begins Elfmar, his voice unsteady. "My nose is …"

"Warty!" shouts a wag.

"Poxy as your Redeless Ethelred!"

"My nose is *downward*. I go on my belly …"

"A worm! Ay, he is a worm!"

"On my belly, and dig into the ground …"

"A *fat* worm!"

"No, wait. I move as directed by the grey enemy of the forest …"

"*Grey enem* …?"

"And by my master and protector …"

"He is the *archbishop's* fat worm!"

"My master and protector who walks stooping at my tail."

Silence, save for the crackle of the fire.

"You must tell them the answer," says Alphege quietly. "And it had better be pleasing to them."

"I am a Plough!" The abbot's voice is strained, and pitched somewhat higher than his usual gruff tones.

There is a pause for thought.

"*Grey enemy of the forest?*" someone says.

Elfmar indicates the greasy bones clutched in several fists.

"The ox," he says. "The ox is the grey enemy of the forest. The ox who draws the plough."

Where the first bone comes from Elfmar can't be sure. He gasps in shock, putting a hand to his overgrown tonsure, feeling for blood. The archbishop is standing beside him now, pushing him with surprising strength towards the ground.

"They are ugly tonight," Alphege mutters. "They have had rather more wine than the meagre pint allowed you by St Benedict. Stay down, and crawl on your belly to the hut there. Save yourself. Lie low and God willing they'll have forgotten about it in the morning."

The good-heartedness of the man sticks even now in the abbot's craw, cloying like a wedge of honeycomb. But he has reason to be glad for it again. *Save yourself* ... And yet again, in spite of that small sense of shame which niggles as it is wont to do, he doesn't hesitate for long, but leaves the archbishop to parry the blows of the tormentors single-handed.

He cringes on the beaten earth floor of the hut with his cowl pulled over his head, stuffing the cloth of it into his ears against the din: the yelling and whooping, the clashing of battleaxes, bursts of song.

In a lull towards dawn Elfmar hears the lonely sound of a bird calling from the marshes. Then the archbishop's voice, weak but still recognizable, although the abbot can't make out what it is he says. And then a Dane speaks harshly:

"It is enough. Make an end."

And one damp thud which sets his stomach heaving.

The revellers are snoring in their quarters. Under the weary eye of a single guard over by the stockade gate, he picks his way through the debris of the night's festivities. Close to the smouldering fire he comes upon the archbishop, or what is left of him: a loose bundle of gory purple wool. Among the litter of drinking cups and ox-bones and axes lies one long wooden pole: an oar. With difficulty Elfmar lifts it and, from a squeamish distance, nudges the archbishop with its blade. Then, with the oar as a prop, he sinks to his knees.

But no prayers will come; instead, his head churns with the

thought: "He knew. He knew it was I who betrayed him and Canterbury. He always knew it."

The abbot kneels for some time, until the day has achieved whatever warmth it will. Then he rises stiffly to his feet and, squinting up through his miserable daze, thinks for a moment that he sees a comet-star, a miraculous apparition like the one he watched forging across the night sky back in the ninety-fifth year of the last century. But after all it is only the sun, pale and jagged through leaves which seem to have branched from the freshly bloodied tip of the Danish oar

Valkyrie

by Nicky Gould

Her song rolls over this dull thud
of perpetual motion, cocoons us
until we can no longer tell
where the rhythm of our bodies ends
and the sound of her begins.
One oarstroke bleeds
into the next, and we reach out –
so many palms pressed
to her skin, so many faces lit
by this changing key.

The music crescendos, pours
our hidden expressions from her lips.
We're caught by the last note, held
between one vibration and the   next,
its liquid sound flowing through hands,
 vertebrae, feet, dying away. Leaving a
thin crack of silence
into which we pour the sharpness of our edges,
 the breeze that surrounds us,
and the shifting seas beneath our feet.

For Love And Money
by Patricia Griffin

I needed money to build my own house back in Denmark. So when the big guy came to my village asking for men to join him on a raid in England, I was quick to step forward. I'd never been in a longship and I was excited by the promise of adventure. But I miss my girlfriend, we're getting married soon. I didn't think we'd be away for so long; I was expecting a quick smash and grab job.

It was rumoured there'd been a tip off from an Abbot; but he didn't warn us of the thick walls surrounding Canterbury. We rammed them for twenty days before someone had a bright idea of using fire as a distraction. I think our friendly monk helped us with that. While the Saxons were frantically putting out the fires we broke through, straight into the town. Talk about all hell breaking out. Of course, our lot were hyped up from drink and the frustration of delay.

"Kill the bastards!" shouted our leader. "Take their valuables, anything you can lay your hands on."

Some women were defiant; you know the type – rich bitches dripping in jewellery, thought themselves too important to be robbed. We got them by the hair, dragged them outside, stripped and speared them. It was easy pickings.

I found a jeweller, stuck him through with my knife and filled a bag with silver bracelets, bangles, gold pendants, gem stones and no end of brooches. Once we'd grabbed the best stuff, we torched the buildings. It wasn't as if they'd need them anymore; the streets were strewn with bodies.

It was like playing a game – we chased a few and slew a few – lost count eventually. I've never heard such a din as those women made, shrieking like wild cats, especially when we snatched their babies from them. I saw one baby tossed onto a warrior's spear; they knifed its mother – shut her up for good. As for the men with their pathetic weapons, they soon learnt they were no match for us.

We didn't kill all of them. If they looked strong or attractive, and didn't put up much resistance we tied them together and frogmarched them to the north gate. Boss had made an arrangement for them to be sold as slaves.

Some houses had little of value, just an odd brooch, like this round one – the decoration's pretty; I pocketed it to give to my girlfriend when I get home. By the time we'd finished searching that house, it was trashed.

In the next house we found a woman with some kids, cowering behind a loom. "Spare us. We've nothing to give you," they pleaded.

"We'll see about that," said my mate.

He snatched the kids and flung them at me. "Hold onto them," he shouted as he stripped the woman, knocked her to the ground and sullied her.

"Your turn," he said to me.

I looked at her face. Her eyes reminded me of my girl when I said goodbye to her, and it was if she was there, saying "What if someone did that to me?"

"No! Leave it," I said. "Let's get to the church." And with that I slung the kids across the room and made a dash for it.

The church gates were closed when we arrived. The monks had barricaded themselves in. We soon solved that problem. We had a good laugh when the fire spread, and mocked the monks when they came running out like ants from a disturbed nest. It didn't take long to loot the place. It had some eye-catching treasure, most of it not much use though, but I thought this silver cup would come in handy, especially at a feast like this. Mind you, the rest will be worth a fortune once it's melted and made into jewellery.

We also grabbed the most important monks, and exchanged

them for a good ransom later. They were hoping to get much more for Elfheah, he being the archbishop, but the old boy forbade anyone to pay it, so we've been lumbered with him for the last seven months. I can't help admiring his spirit; I wouldn't risk death for anyone.

I don't know why they've brought him out of prison tonight; the poor devil can hardly stand up. The warriors over there are going berserk, too much drink I suppose. And now they're chucking bones at him.

Bloody hell! Thorkell's finished him off with his axe.

Well, at least he's no longer suffering, and I can drink to seeing my girl again soon.

It's strange how the wine in this cup now tastes like blood.

Gold Is The Colour
by Jo Field

White and carrying as a billowed sail
is the soul of a good man. With the death
of summer and the days docked, Alphege
and his followers are holed up in the city,
holding out against the Danish threat.

Red: betrayal by a feckless abbot.
Marauders wade knee-deep in red; throats
rasp and gargle with it, gutters run scarlet.
Carcasses of children serve as trophies
spitted on Danish spears.

Black clouds shroud this bitter autumn
wracked and ragged with screams. Tears
of bruised women spill like molten lead.
Was there a heart to find in Thurkill's men
it would be black.

Give us gold! The chorus of the Danes.
Alphege won't be ransomed:
The gold I give you is the word of God he says,
 but what can be bought with words?
He doesn't know if he'll see Canterbury again.

Grey: the old man stands immured on deck
under a stony sky. Heavy oars scythe
clean cuts in the sea. Dragon prows
carve through the polished granite estuary
reaching for haven like migrating birds.

Danes rediscover their barbaric hearts
revived in the wineskin dark of winter nights.
Then ox-bone and axe-haft drive all colour
from the hostage flesh and that frail body
lies battered and broken on the ground.

Green miracle. Green hope.
An oar dipped in the martyr's blood
        bursts into leaf.
Ordained as surely as man's greed
another spring comes round.

1012 – The Miller's Arms – Backroom Banter

by Jeremy Langrish

… a bloody farce that was, that Oxford charter, licence for a free-for-all to nobble the gits – Aethelread shit-for-brains dropped a right bollock there! They did the little darlings in, didn't know about the bird, the king of Sweden's sister.

That was it for starters. We'd got their goat. The big bloke Torkell came and ran amok, raised merry hell around the place, but London's lads stood firm. And that Ulfkettle, har har. Got himself an army of poofs. Right Essex girls they were, the first thing they did was scarper! All over Anglia, blood and fire.

Then the buggers came back here – and we'd been getting on alright, they'd struck a deal for cash before, but they were coming back for more – they wanted Alfi's stash. Tried to take our Kentish stronghold, Our Lady's Birthday when it started, they really didn't stand a chance. Had to wait till Mikklemas, when pisspot Aelfmaer let them. A really scary time that was, they strung us blokes up by the bollocks, and hauled the girls off by their hair and burned them, yeah – they even piked the babies. They carted off the well-to-do, the clergymen were flush, that Minster tart, she'd got some wonga, reckon that they got it too. They never took that wet fart Aelfmaer, let him off for helping, hung on to The Bishop though, tried everything to get the dosh, but Alfi never coughed. They threatened to kill him if we didn't pay. Got their come-uppance when they all got the shits. Snuffing it all over the place. But it never slowed them down …

… and on the Sunday after Easter, when they all got pissed they brung old Alfi out to have another go, and someone axed him in the head, and that, said Jack, was that …

… What a state! … A bloody shambles … that's what we've paid our taxes for … Hey ho … Yeah, I'll have another thanks … Unread Aethelread. Couldn't run a pissup in a brewery …

The Siege Of Canterbury – September 1011

by Ruth Henderson

One thousand years ago they came
To rape and pillage, kill and maim.
The townsfolk hid in fear.
They closed the gates and manned the walls
Then trembled as they heard the calls
Of Danes, as they came near.

They could do nought but wait and pray
On this, the Blessed Virgin's Day,
And find what was their fate.
For three long weeks they kept them out
But then they heard a dreadful shout –
Aelfmaer had raised the gate!

And so it was on Michaelmas Day
Vikings rushed in to slash and slay
And plunder all they could.
The monks were killed, Cathedral burned,
Houses were robbed, chests overturned –
They could not be withstood.

Then Canterbury's narrow lanes
Were overrun by warrior Danes
And people fled in fear.
They hid behind old Roman walls
In dread of the bloodcurdling calls
That came from far and near.

The fearsome Vikings ran amok
Killing; the young for slaves they took,
Or tore some limb from limb.
Alphege they bound and prisoner made
Until a ransom could be paid –
A high price placed on him.

For seven months they held him fast
But when they realised at last
All ransom he decried
Ox-heads and bones at him they threw,
And thus the saintly man they slew – '
Twas thus good Alphege died.

One thousand years have passed since then –
In names we still remember when
To Danes the townsfolk cowed.
Now tourists climb the 'Dane John' Mound
And from that height see all around
The city standing proud.

Deliver Us From Evil

by Marilyn Donovan

Canterbury Cathedral, 29th September 1011

Fæder ure þu þe eart on heofonum. The monks huddled near the altar behind Brother Eadmer have lasped into the vernacular, wits addled with terror so they are trapped mumbling the same phrase over and over. *Fæder ure þu, Fæder ure þu, Fæder, Fæder,* as if the collective act of invoking the Almighty's name will snag His attention, urge a divine hand to reach down from the firmament and pluck them to safety.

Eadmer, the monastery's infirmarer, halts as he moves through the nave tending the panicked and injured townsfolk who have sought sanctuary. Frowning, he turns to catch the eye of one of the novices, signing for him to lead the brothers away from their fruitless circling. Lyfing, his face milk-pale and closed with fear, nods his understanding. Pushing his shoulders back and lifting his chin, he draws a trembling breath. Then, eyes unfocussed and staring straight ahead with the effort of mastering the shudders unmanning him, his voice rises above the brothers' muttered incantation pulling them gently on: *Si þin nama gehalgod, Hallowed be Thy name.*

And the monks, after a pause, draw strength from his strength, follow, pour more vigour into their words, though their throats be tight with fear. First one, then others, till most have wrenched their minds away from the horror waiting hours, minutes perhaps, ahead, fastening their thoughts instead on the glory and comfort of Him they beseech. *Tobecume þin rice,* Thy kingdom come. The recitation has become slower, measured, more coherent and the melée of townsfolk crowded round them cross themselves as if in acknowledgement, bow their heads. Some begin moving their lips in silent accompaniment.

Waving remonstrations aside with an impatient flick of the hand, Ælfheah *arcebiscop* has ordered the great cathedral doors to be left open till the last moment that the town's denizens may flee hither to safety. So now the doors, hewn and carved from solid Kentish oak, adorned with intricate iron hinges and good metal rivets, stand wide. Late September sunlight floods in, laying golden fingers across the bodies of the shocked and maimed, the newly-made widows and mewling babies, the children petrified into silence, the separated and lost, the bewildered elderly, the sick and afraid, rich and poor crowded there.

The Danes have been laying siege to the town this past one and twenty days, its homes and lodging houses, monasteries and convents, stables and alleyways crammed to capacity, its population swollen with the tide of refugees fleeing ahead of the heathens' steady advance. Serf, lord, miller, tanner, freeman, fisherman, slave: all have come, a panicked rout herding their families and animals before them, their chattels loaded on rumbling carts or strapped to their backs.

The autumn breeze carries the stench of burning as the infidel horde touch fire to all before them. And more: a confused din like unto the Apocrypha where grumble still too far away to separate screams, moans, yells, supplications for mercy, the clash and ring of metal. Somewhere a building slides and thumps to earth, burnt out.

Ælfheah *arcebiscop* has walked out into the midst of the fighting, must be somewhere in that hell of lunge and thrust and hack, the ineffectual parry as a two-handed axe is swung, children cut down in sight of their parents, old people broken under the hooves of panicked cattle, the smell of freshly let blood. Eadmer imagines his slight figure, at first dignified in his mitre and crozier, then grown desperate at the horror wreaked around him, reaching his arms in supplication to brute after brute, pleading for the slaughter to cease.

Perhaps he is holding out promise of the cathedral's treasures, the gold censers and silver-spouted jugs, the jewelled crosses and shining chalices, the gold æstels and carved reliquaries, the crystals, fine filigree and enamelled cloisonné, leather bags heavy with silver pennies and gold mancuses. If so, he wastes his breath: the Northmen's blood lust is up and coursing, they will not be satisfied till all lie slain but the rich and influential taken for ransom. Only then will they turn to thoughts of plunder, to tumbling holy relics from their ivory caskets and ripping the jewel-set covers from the great gospel books, defiling all with their bloodstained hands.

Gewurþe þin willa on eorðan swa swa on heofonum, Thy will be done on earth as it is in heaven. They must, Eadmer thinks, have sinned mightily to deserve such punishment. Hadn't Ælfheah *arcebiscop* himself been telling them so, quoting often from the Sermo Lupi delivered by Wulfstan, *arcebiscop* of Eorwic, to the great Council three years before. And yet, deep within, he finds it difficult to believe a just God would visit such cruel chastisement.

The Northmen have been camped outside the town for one and twenty days, terrifying the citizens within with their jigging and grimacing, their waving of axes and spears, the rhythmic thump of sword pommel on wooden shield. They say their blades are forged by dwarves, have names, Widowmaker and the like, are tempered in the blood of babies for strength.

Eadmer *læce* has used the time well. Though praying the walls will hold, as they have throughout history, fathers proudly praising their stoutness to sons through generation after generation, he knew the slaughter would be terrible if they were breached and has laid his plans. He has worked long hours in his infirmary, overseeing the gathering and steeping of herbs, brewing of draughts, mashing of poultices, the tearing of good linen sheets into lengths of bandage.

He has, too, enlisted the help of monks hand-picked for their practical ways and staunchness of heart: Brother Cenwulf the monastery's jovial cook, whose stomach does not heave at the smell of butchered meat; Brother Plegmund who minds the stables, is wise and patient in nurturing beasts; lantern-jawed Brother Leofric, whose saintly calm has surely marked him out for heaven. Excused from solitary meditation, he has trained them in the rudimentaries of physicianship. And now, though they may not be *rihtlæces*, as he is, they are proving handy in tending the dreadful wounds presented. For five hours now they have threaded quietly through the crowd, assessing, setting relatives to press down hard to stem bleeding, neighbours to fashion and tighten ligatures, tipping flagons filled with herbal draughts to trembling lips that the injured may drink and ease their pain. He has bid them not waste time on the mortally wounded or those already passed to glory but to mutter a hasty blessing, lay hands on a shoulder in comfort and move away to minister to those who can be saved.

Thy will be done. Perhaps he was wrong to plan thus mitigating God's vengeance, perhaps he should instead have submitted meekly, instructed the monks only to administer the last rights, pray over the dead? But no, in his heart he cannot believe it.

The moment word was sent of a fire set sufficient to weaken the town's defences, he caused the sick and elderly already in his care to be moved into the cathedral's nave and lain behind the altar, though he doubts the Northmen, worshippers of fierce pagan gods, will heed the laws of sanctuary. He has had, too, three of the oak refectory tables hauled in and set down near windows, the better to see and treat the maimed. Buckets of water freshly drawn from the well stand alongside.

Behind him he hears Lyfing's voice floating above the babel. *Urne gedæghwamlican hlaf syle us to dæg,* Give us this day our daily bread. The novice would, Eadmer reflects, have risen to become a great church leader had he survived the slaughter rolling steadily towards them.

And forgyf us ure gyltas, swa swa we forgyfað urum gyltendum, And forgive us our trespasses, as we forgive those who trespass against us. The new arrivals have brought a rumour that Ælfmaer *abbod* has betrayed them, he whose life was once saved by the holy Ælfheah. No doubt, they whisper grimly, in exchange for safe passage. *And ne gelæd þu us on costnunge,* And lead us not into temptation. Eadmer stems the urge to curse St Augustine's abbot, mutters instead a brief intercession for a soul bound for the vilest torments of a cold, cold hell.

Outside, the sounds of strife are getting closer. It is possible, now, to pick out individual voices wailing, begging for mercy, screaming for their loved ones to run faster, faster, to leave them to their fate and save themselves. They can hear too the Northmen yelling hideous curses in their harsh, throaty guttural, urging themselves on to yet more slaughter. Horses neigh their terror, cattle moan in their distress deep and low and urgent, a runaway cart clatters over cobbles. And through it all weaves the crackle and spit of flames as houses, workshops, stables, storerooms are touched with fiery brands.

The small night door leading to the dorter was shut and locked when the monks first filed into the cathedral. It is time now to sign that the great oak doors be closed, the iron key turned, the bolts shot, massive metal bars slotted into place. The last inside is an old man, one arm dangling useless from a grievous shoulder wound, mouth pressed close in pain so that his lips are blue.

The flow of air cut off, the stench inside rises, a miasma of stinking breath and the festering *swát* of bodies left unwashed in the overcrowding since the siege was laid, a ripeness of faeces and *cúmicge* and vomit as bowels slacken, bladders loosen at the hurled rocks, the crazed pounding and blood-stopping oaths of the heathen on the other side. And something worse, the crystal-cold, knife-sharp reek of terror, pure and unadulterated, as those within realize that here, now, they are sealed in, there is no way out.

For a moment Eadmer's lungs refuse to draw in breath, he loses focus, staggers, is caught and held by kindly hands. He shakes his head to clear the mist, bends the full strength of his will to pulling the heated iron from the brazier, to cauterising the stump of the girl on the table before him. By the time he leans back, the furious battering outside has stopped, the snarled fury fallen quiet. Inside, the wailing of the women, the howling of children peter and fade, leaving a queasy silence into which trickle the groans of the injured, the sighs of the dying. Somewhere near him a baby whimpers, is instinctively put to the breast.

And now, through the conjoined reek of filth and fear and seared flesh, the overflowing buckets of excrement placed discreetly behind screens, twines another, more sinister note. At first he catches only threads, then ribbons, thinks it must be drifting in through the broken windows, but soon it is snaking unmistakable through the nave in roiling swathes. Smoke. The Danes have fired the building! Soon the air will thicken and choke, the thick roof-beams will catch and flare, pelt them with burning embers, the lead roofing will melt and drop in bright coins more deadly than any acid burn. They will be forced to unbar the doors, to stampede out onto the waiting swords.

Somewhere in the distance, in that one moment before the screaming starts and men become maddened beasts, he hears Lyfing's voice, lone and fluting now but groping doggedly to the end. *Ac alys us of yfele.* Deliver us from evil.

Palm Sunday
by Gillian Laker

Portents have been
ignored or misread
for our ceremonies
are different this year.

Not sweet fronds
tender under hoof
but the iron smell of
ox blood and hair.

Not the delicate ransom
of our Lord
but the hollow ring
of Danegeld.

Not the Son but the sun-
set of a Norse echo.
Not the tree of Jesse
 but Yggdrasil.

My captors move against
stone certainties
missing their heroes
and the world-ash,

singing harsh songs
and breaking my bones
with the gnawed relics
of their feasting.

Until an axe returns me
to the quiet space
of my hermitage
and shows me

the slap and swell
of the North Sea
slowly losing faith
in its own Gods.

1011 – The Fall Of The Spirit Of Canterbury

by Lorraine Hayward

I am the spirit that dwells in the walls that ring this city. This city the sainted Augustine blessed. In Christ's name, I am appointed guardian of those within Canterbury's bounds. I hold them to me, shield and comfort them, offer shelter and peace. But they know not of me. They see not my arms embracing their borders or behold in the towers my defiant stance. They see only my line of stone and timber, my gates and my locks. They have faith that they will hold. They must have faith. For my spirit will hold my wall for long as their spirit does not quake.

For many centuries of our Lord, I have stood witness to this faith. I see and I hear and I garner my strength from the hearts of those within and the many masters I have served. I count them now. Twenty-ninth is Alphege. I fear for my Archbishops – they bear the burdens of God. Their times will determine their mettle. Some will pass in their beds; some will die at the hands of sin. What times have we now?

For three score years I hear rumour and panic as men pass by my feet. In taverns they yarn of Viking lords, of Olaf and Swein. Of ships sailing south, fearsomely figured at stem and stern, bearing hosts arrayed in hauberk and helm, armed with sword and shield and mighty axe. Travellers bring news of wasted Strathclyde, of destruction and pillage in far Bernicia, of fire and plunder in northern castles and southern ports. Their horses tremble in telling of brethren enslaved, ridden swift and hard 'cross terrorised land. I hear the boasts of the rooks who rest in my battlements and crow of their feasts with the hawks and the wolves, who gorge and bloat on the carrion-fields. I hear of battle and burning, of blood and slaughter, of the cries of children plucked from the breast, and the sorrow of women. I hear of a king unready, of counsel un-prevailing and of ransomed peace. Danegeld must be paid – £10,000, £16,000, £24,000. Taxes rise and proclamations are made – men of eight hides must find helmet and breastplate, men possessed of 310 hides to provide galley or skiff.

But neither arms nor coin deter their bloody progress and now on the eve of St Mary's day, once more this scourge is at my door. We have withstood before, my walls and I, when Thorkell came two years before. Tall he was, and strong. He stood before us and roared his demand. And £3,000 bought safety. Now they demand again and at my gates a heathen horde digs in. Their lord camps with his henchmen at my northern tower and sets forth his terms. "Listen to us", he cries. "If you wish to escape death, heed us. We seek the freedom of your city, nothing more. We do not desire your blood. Let us pass in and have no fear".

In my towers gather the men-folk of the city. Brave fellows and lads. These are not warriors. They are tanners and weavers, chandlers and merchants, servants and slaves. But their anger charges them. "No. We will not let you in. This is our city. We have built and we have prospered. It will not be yours." I feel their courage swell my stone with strength and with vigour my foundations grasp the earth anew. But the Viking lord laughs and raises his sword. "Then your city is forfeit and your deaths secured. Whom we do not slaughter, we will starve. Look to your God."

He drops his sword in command and upon a fearsome roar a single spear pierces the sky, arcing high above me and dropping into the belly of the city. As its head slices into the mud of the market place, all eyes in Canterbury turn outwards in a stupor of stilled breath and dreadful anticipation. And the horde falls upon my walls. Their siege towers trundle forward. Their catapults rain stone and fire. Their bodies swarm and grapple upon my sides. Stone splits and timber splinters. Swords swing and stab, axes heft. Blood and sweat flow. Heads and limbs are broken. "Stand fast, stand fast," I urge. And the men of the city hold firm, and while the air fills with the clamour of combat and the agony of the wounded, from within the city a sweet chant arises. Pure voices in plain song which soar heaven-ward, dispelling the evil cacophony resounding around my walls. I feel my innards reverberate with melodious praises and the light tread of Archbishop Alphege, as he leads his deacons through the stairs of my north tower. I feel his feet plant on the battlement where he raises the Cross as a standard against this unholy rout. And his deacons raise their voices higher and higher in a melancholic plea to God and peace. And for a sweet, short moment the tumult is paused as blood-stained warriors turn their eyes to Alphege's call.

"Blessed is the Lord our God." His voice is strong, betraying no fear in the face of this godless foe. "He will not suffer us to submit our church to your hands. We will defend our faith and he will deliver us. Cease your assault, repent of your wickedness, and God will forgive you. Heed our Lord not and you will be punished." But the Viking does not fear our God. He has the strength of Thor and Odin still coursing in his veins. And with a clash of metal and flesh, their assault is renewed. My lord Alphege drops to his knees in prayer and amidst the showers of arrow and rock, his deacons fearing for his life lead him into my shelter. But the Cross they leave high on my battlement, silhouetting the faith of the city against the sky and by nightfall the assault is repelled.

And the next morn it begins again. And the next, and the next. For two score days the enemy in turn sits then attacks, sits then attacks. They jeer. They cajole. They promise and they threaten. They are both fearless and numerous. And within, the water sours and food dwindles, the bodies pile and the city stinks, and fires are quenched and ravages mended in the daily round of hostage, blood and terror as the city holds true.

But misery stalks the streets of Canterbury. I hear of dissent and debate, and lights burn in the cathedral and the meeting house long into the nights. The ealdors who have much to lose of wealth and power will not be gainsaid in the defence of the city. The king's men who watch the mint will not surrender their post without fight. My master and his followers who seek to defend the cathedral in the Lord's name implore, "God will heed our prayers. He will not forsake us." And the powerful fall deaf to the pleas of the women and of those who raise common love above valour and glory, wealth and witness, in God's name or the king's. "Our children are starving, our old people weaken. Our sons and husbands and fathers are slain. No silver, or cloth or standing can be sufficient price for their souls. And what is your church but stone and mortar? What of our flesh and blood? We beseech you lords, open the gates, bring an end to our toil. If not, who will save us?" And I must bear their sorrow. I grieve as they twist and turn in their agonies, are divided and wretched in their needs and their faith. For I am charged with only one task: to hold while my charges hold. And to my pain, I am at once their saviour and their downfall.

On the eve of the 20th day, when quiet is marked only by the wailing of babes and the weeping of the weak, I see a shadow pass under my northern gate. A man walks from my care and into the camp of the Viking lord. The visitor seeks parley but I hear from the enemy only false promises of safety and respite, reward and release. "We want only leave of the town – we wish no harm. Your children will be fed, your sick will be tended. Your God does not wish your suffering. It is the pig-headedness of your leaders, seeking glory and a martyr's fate. Let us in, man of God, let us in. Let us in and save your flock." And the archdeacon returns to the city.

I feel my power quake. I hold no sway over the treachery of men. And in the early hours of the following morn, as the sun rises casting a fire of red and gold across the sky, I feel heat arising in my easterly tower and I perceive at once the desperate betrayal. I summon all my strength to the tower's defence but the flames are too fierce and my limbs tremble, my shoulders fall and my roots begin to loose their hold. The tower walls, already battered and broken, crumble and shatter, and a hole gapes through to the enemy's blockade where the Viking horde waits to enter. And they swarm through with a bloodcurdling cry and eyes which betray any vision of mercy.

Too few city-men survive to defend their wives and children, their livestock and houses. It takes but a short time to lay waste to the city, to plunder what they will and fire what remains, their vicious progression through the streets and the lanes marked in a bloody wake of wasted humanity. I see them. I see them all. There lies Eadgard and his son, limbs hacked and heads cloven in a last hopeless defence. Over there is Iuwine, her body still shielding those of her once- blossoming daughters. In his bed, old Stefn lies, an axe blow delivering him from a lingering starvation. Death follows death after death; sorrowful testament to the evil of men and, to my shame, the breach of my walls and so my duty.

My faltering spirit pursues this trail of misery and murder to the city's heart where, in God's holy strength, the cathedral stands still. But I fear it offers no sanctuary. The Abbess Leofrun is seized, Bishop Godwine is captured. And before the altar I see them take Alphege as he makes his last genuflexion. He is a pretty prize and they will seek to barter with his life. But I know my lord. In God's name he will forbear their demands. They will kill him. But the Lord will demand that there is not sorrow but praise in his passing. For his death will be made saintly, and his witness will strengthen the city's faith in our God. That faith will rebuild my walls and Canterbury will become great and holy again. For what is the Christian church but a bastion of sacrifice?

But those whose sacrifice reaps no acclaim? The common-folk of Canterbury? Their torments will pass silently into a dark history. No more. And I? I will persevere in my watch until my strength is wrought anew: a pitiful safeguard of the forsaken corpses and the dogs that scavenge in the ruins of the city.

May the Lord deliver us.

A Witness-worth Of Words
by Ron Ogilvie

Listen –
The wolves out-with the worried walls
Have us held fast:
As water ices
We are let to lie,
To sere in this saltern
With our un-fostered kith.

One day, they
Will gather us in,
Just a heriot's hollow crop,
But now we are
Left to our lather,
No meal, no meat
Only our stitching starve.

We have our priest,
The straddle of our city:
Whilst we have him
We can suck on ox bones,
Bite birds from the air
And drink our drench
And as we wane
We'll sing.

What say you, Aelfmaer?
How will their axes answer then?

Consultancy, Formatting, Graphics and Cover Design

by

Hot Monkey Publishing

www.hotmonkeypublishing.com

www.ingramcontent.com/pod-product-compliance
Lightning Source LLC
Chambersburg PA
CBHW072045170626
46811CB00008B/3173